CARR CLIFTON
CALIFORNIA
MAGNIFICENT WILDERNESS

PHOTOGRAPHY BY CARR CLIFTON

WESTCLIFFE PUBLISHERS, INC. ENGLEWOOD, COLORADO

CONTENTS

International Standard Book Number:
ISBN 0-942394-78-X
Copyright, Photographs and Text: Carr Clifton,
1988
Designer: Gerald Miller Simpson/Denver
Typographer: Edward A. Nies
Printer: Dai Nippon Printing Company, Ltd.,
Tokyo, Japan
Publisher: Westcliffe Publishers, Inc.
2650 South Zuni Street
Englewood, Colorado 80110

*First frontispiece: Fresh water rill patterns in the sand,
Trinidad State Beach*

*Second frontispiece: Tenaya Lake, within the alpine
domain of Yosemite National Park*

*Third frontispiece: Rhododendron blossoms and
redwood trees, Lady Bird Johnson Grove, Redwood
National Park*

*Title page: A solitary blossom of salmonberry rests
upon redwood sorrel*

*Right: Rime ice consumes the boughs of a digger pine,
Trinity Alps*

PREFACE

is a photographer's heaven. I once made my home along California's north coast in Trinidad while a friend finished her studies at Humboldt State University. There I became attuned to the rhythms of the weather and the seasons, and their effect on my rhythms and moods.

I remember going down to the same beach every evening to enjoy its colors and patterns. Every trip to the misty shoreline revealed something new — it was never the same as the day before, but neither was I. I made it a point to focus on the many various realms of seashore. After I'd become accustomed to the broad, powerful seascape, I turned my attention to other ways of seeing. I looked down and photographed patterns at my feet. I watched the waxing and waning tides and the waves varnishing the rocks with a glossy glow. I saw foam from the surf dance across the beach in the wind. I was becoming intimate with my environment and beginning to imagine that I could convey all I observed through the lens of my camera.

One exceptionally calm evening after photographing the last sunset hues on the glowing sand, I glanced at the sun as it was dipping below the horizon and couldn't believe what I was seeing. It was the fabled Emerald-green Snap of Light Phenomenon (my term) that sometimes occurs when the sun sets or rises over oceans. I had heard people mention it on beach hikes or around a roaring camp fire, but had always dismissed it as an optical illusion. Yet here it was, very real, and then within ten seconds — gone.

I was so stunned by the hypnotic green glow that I didn't even attempt to re-assemble the camera for a shot. I knew then not every experience could be translated on film. I preserve this grand phenomenon within myself as a private, retinal image.

Perhaps to some people the images on these pages may be as awe-inspiring and unexpected as the Emerald-green Snap of Light Phenomenon was to me on the north coast of California. As long as there is wildness, we may witness such astonishing beauty. The preservation of Earth's living surface is up to us. Whether pristine lakes tucked away from the bustling cities or noble oaks along a busy highway, patterns of leaves blowing in the wind or the spine of entire mountain ranges, we must recognize and defend the natural environment. We cannot continue to see the world as just so many resources created for human consumption, and gobble up everything in our path without serious regard for the fate of the Earth. When we must develop areas for human use, we must do so with forethought, not lack of thought. We need to forge an environmental ethic, a social commitment to protect the land, air and water from avoidable human abuses. Without such a commitment we will continue to plunder our surroundings. Books of photographs such as this one will reveal only a history rather than be a reminder of the living wilderness available to all who are willing to seek it.

Carr Clifton

Sandstone concretions, Borrego Badlands,
Anza-Borrego Desert State Park

THE
SIERRA NEVADA
& MONO LAKE

Foxtail pine preside over Kern Canyon,
Sequoia National Park

The fecund and the sterile: flora of Spring, Ansel Adams Wilderness; Isosceles and Columbine Peaks from Dusy Basin, Kings Canyon National Park

Nature's studies in form: the microcosm of squirreltail barley and rare shapes of sand tufa, on the edge of Mono Lake

Overleaf: Sunset casts its color over Thousand Island Lake, Ansel Adams Wilderness

The Great Western Divide from Franklin Pass,
Sequoia National Park

Reflections of Autumn, Lights Creek,
northern Sierra Nevada Mountains

Contrasts of nature: sunrise reflects upon glacially polished granite in the Hoover Wilderness and upon the surface of Mono Lake

Overleaf: Lone Pine Peak seen through a quartz monzonite arch, Alabama Hills

Autumn foliage: sedge grass and willow shoots,
and vine maple behind a pine snag, along Indian Creek,
northern Sierra Nevada Mountains

*Similitudes of color: sunset at Tuolumne Meadows,
Yosemite National Park; the pink of Lewis's monkey
flower, Hoover Wilderness*

Boulders and Finger Peaks, Yosemite National Park
Tumbleweed and tufa, Dusk, Mono Lake

Deliberation and alacrity: Indian Creek, northern Sierra
Nevada Mountains; fresh water below Mt. Ritter and
Banner Peak, Ansel Adams Wilderness

Overleaf: Thunderstorm clouds over Tenaya Lake,
Yosemite National Park

*A contrast of season: squirreltail barley in the wetness of
Spring and the aridity of Summer, around Mono Lake*

*Evening light: cattails in Mono Lake and lodgepole pine
in the Ansel Adams Wilderness*

Overleaf: Morning light, Mono Lake

Tufa formations against storm clouds, Mono Lake
The Great Western Divide, Sequoia National Park

COAST &
REDWOODS

Ferns, moss, and fresh water along the coast of Big Sur

A contrast of size within the forest: silhouettes
of prodigious redwood trees; diminutive trillium and
redwood sorrel, Redwood National Park

Surf-pounded redwood at Hidden Beach,
Redwood National Park, and surf-sculptured rock
at Garrapata Beach

Overleaf: Sunset and low tide, Trinidad State Beach

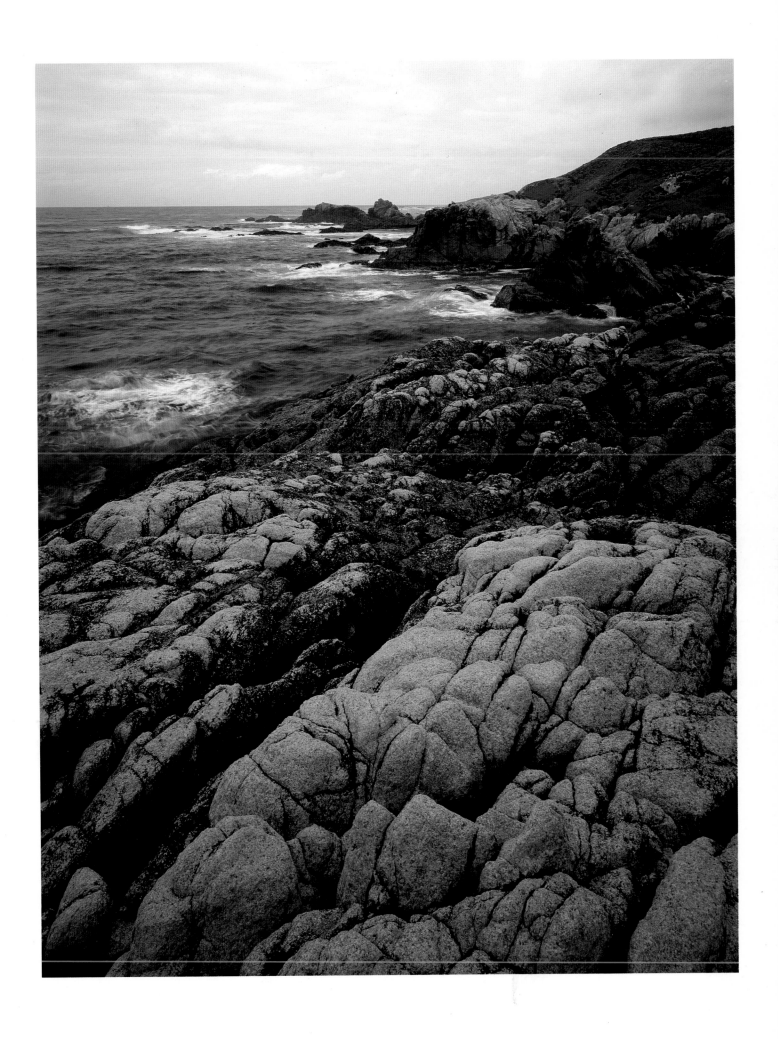

Evening rays on beach boulders, Trinidad State Beach
Douglas's iris, Prairie Creek Redwoods State Park

Motion and a lack of it: surf on Garrapata Beach;
dwarf Oregon grape leaves, north coast

Overleaf: Redwoods drink from coastal fog, Lady Bird
Johnson Grove, Redwood National Park

Roses and grass erase old boundaries,
northern California coast

Daisies and sea stacks, northern California coast

The golden glow of sunset gilds both rocks and sand at ocean's edge, Trinidad State Beach

Overleaf: Once tame roses consume man's work and nature repossesses its ground, northern California coast

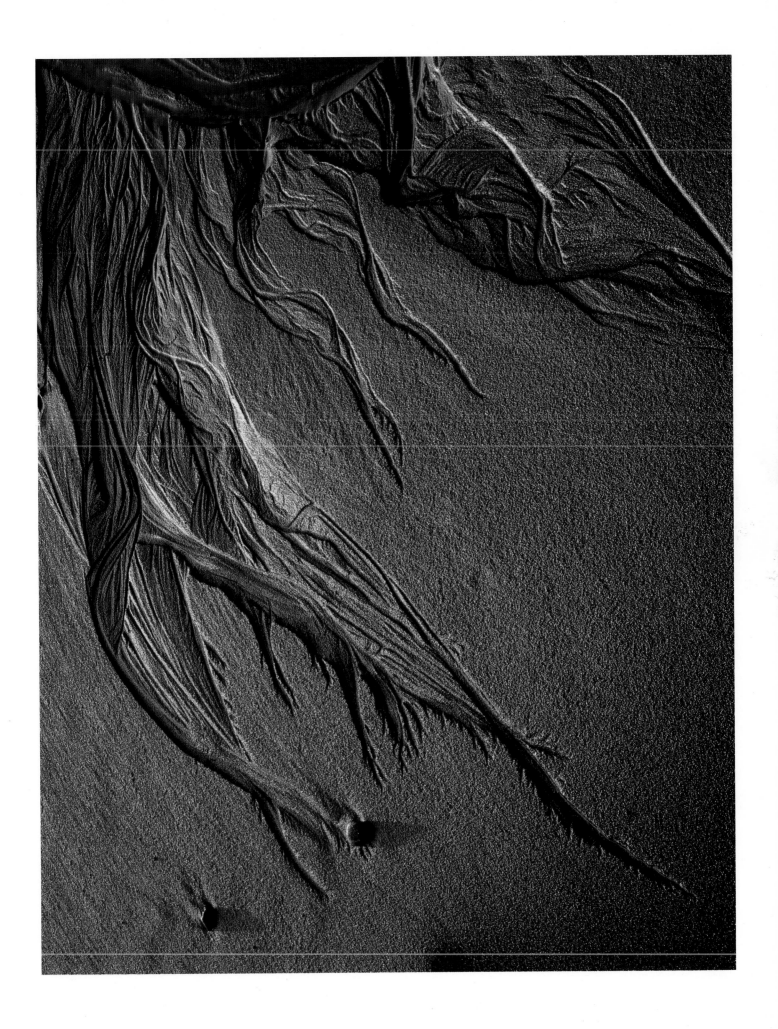

DESERTS

Eroded cliffs manifest their form in evening light,
Red Rock Canyon State Park

Native fan palms, Anza-Borrego Desert State Park

Mesquite Flat Sand Dunes, Death Valley
National Monument

Kelso Dunes and the Granite Mountains, Mohave Desert

Salt flats, near Badwater, Death Valley
National Monument

Denizens of the desert: fierce desert agave,
Anza-Borrego Desert State Park; beavertail cactus,
Joshua Tree National Monument

Overleaf: Morning light at Mesquite Flat Sand Dunes,
Death Valley National Monument

The aridity of desert in both plant and earth: the Borrego Badlands and native fan palm, Anza-Borrego Desert State Park

In an arid environment exist both form and color:
patterns of agave and the yellow of brittle-bush

Overleaf: A storm approaches over
the Chocolate Mountains

The diversity of spring flora,
Anza-Borrego Desert State Park

Barrel cactus, Whipple Mountains

*Illuminated by the desert sun: jumping cholla cactus and
the surface of beavertail cactus, Whipple Mountains*

OAKS, HILLS, &
VOLCANOES

California poppies color the landscape,
Montana de Oro State Park

Oak, Mount Diablo State Park

Mt. Lassen, Lassen Volcanic National Park

Overleaf: Oaks and green grass of the California winter,
Mount Diablo State Park

Elusive moments in time: sunrise and fresh snow, Coast Range; oaks in fog, Mount Diablo State Park

The Santa Lucia Range, Ventana Wilderness

McArthur-Burney Falls, McArthur-Burney Falls Memorial Park

Overleaf: Bulrush stand through ice in a frozen pond,
Honey Lake Wildlife Area

A contrast of season: blue oaks of Spring and metamorphic rock, central Sierra Nevada foothills; big leaf maple in Autumn, southern Cascade Range

*From the ferocity of a dormant volcano to the tranquility
of wildflowers on a hillside: Mt. Shasta and valley lupine
in the Carmel Valley*

Morning light, Lava Beds National Monument

Oak and lichen patterns on basalt boulders,
northern California foothills

Cow clover, Table Mountain
Fog-shrouded oak on Fremont Peak, Fremont Peak State Park
Overleaf: Crimson clover, Klamath Range

Sunset, central Sierra Nevada foothills
Sunrise, Honey Lake Wildlife Area

Morning glory, Montana de Oro State Park
Basalt boulders, Bidwell Park, northern California

Macrocosm and microcosm — nature's diversity:
Basalt boulders and live oak, northern California
foothills; wild daisies, Plumas County

TECHNICAL
INFORMATION

The images within this book were made with either a Tachihara 4″ × 5″ field view camera or a Toyo 4″ × 5″ field view camera. Lenses of 90mm, 135mm, 180mm, 240mm, and 300mm focal lengths were used.

Ektachrome 64 and Fujichrome 50 daylight transparency films were used exclusively. Red color correcting filters were used to correct for a cyan imbalance in the Ektachrome film.

Exposures were calculated with a Gossen Luna-Pro light meter using both a gray card and values of light in the landscape. Apertures varied from f5.6 to f64. Exposures ranged from 1/60 second to about 30 seconds.

Valley oaks on ancient lava flow,
northern California foothills